HOW TO
Dream

YOUR LUCKY

LOTTO
NUMBERS

HOW TO
Dream
YOUR LUCKY
LOTTO
NUMBERS

RAOUL MALTAGLIATI

BARNES
&NOBLE
BOOKS
NEW YORK

2000 Barnes & Noble Books

ISBN 0-7607-1768-0 *casebound*
ISBN 0-7607-1769-9 *paperback*

Printed and bound in the United States of America

00 01 02 03 04 MC 9 8 7 6 5 4 3 2 1
00 01 02 03 04 MP 9 8 7 6 5 4 3 2 1

RRD-H

TABLE OF CONTENTS

FOREWORD

BY GENNARO ESPOSITO

A primma vuota che incuntrai. (I wish the words of Gennaro could be translated maintaining the spontaneity and the harmony of the original Neapolitan dialect).

The first time that I met Raoul, trying yet to be nice with my visitors, as I usually do, I thought: "Oh my God, here is another one of those busybodies (*ficcanaso*) from up north who come down to study us and our practices as if we were a tribe from the jungle. They always forget that we belong to the same country and our civilization is as old as theirs, if not older."

Then, we talked about one hour, and I must say that I had to change my opinion about him. When he left we were almost friends, and the second and third time that we saw each other, we became real friends. I appreciated very much the open mind and the humility with which he approached a subject which many people, especially from the technologically advanced north, laugh at. When I asked why he was able to differentiate himself from the average skeptic, Raoul answered that, in spite of all the most recent studies, there were too many things which we did not know about the connection between our dreams and our waking life. Maybe the practice of a Dream Interpreter, as I am considered to be, could uncover one of the keys to this connection and it was worth being taken into consideration.

A few years later Raoul called me from Florence to ask if I had anything against his writing a book for the Americans about my interpretation of dreams and my method to extract the lotto numbers from them. I told him that he could do whatever he liked, but I thought it was a crazy idea, and that the people on the other side of the ocean would think that I and my believers were a bunch of nuts. He said not to worry, that for him it would be enough to sell the book just to the Americans of Italian descent. I did not worry: as a matter of fact I forgot the whole matter completely until he sent me a copy of the book.

This year, when Raoul told me that the first printing of the book was sold out and he asked me to write a foreword to the second printing, I was absolutely amazed. Then, when he told me that the book had been translated in Hungarian, the thought that my ideas could have been debated in Budapest was so unbelievable that it made me laugh. God only knows what kind of link there is between Neapolitans and Hungarians!

Or maybe there is a link. Perhaps it is time for everyone to realize that nationalities are detachable labels, and once they are removed, everybody finds themselves with the same feelings, the same fears, and the same hopes.

DREAM YOUR WAY
TO SUCCESS

LOTTO: WHAT IS IT?

Saturday night, 11 P.M., TV news.

Millions of Americans reach for a tiny piece of paper with a few numbers printed on it, all with the same hope: maybe this time they made it!

But what is this crazy thing? Why do people bet their money when no horses and dogs are running, when no football games are being played, and no fighters are breaking each other's faces? What is going on?

Thanks for being concerned, but we don't need all that mess anymore: Lotto is here!

It is very easy to play, maybe a little less easy to win; but who cares about the odds as long as Luck is going to be a Lady on Saturday night?

With few differences from state to state, all you have to do to play the game is to guess the three or more numbers that are drawn each week at random by each state's Lottery.

You fill in a form with the numbers you choose, pay your bet of, let's say, a dollar. The state puts all the dollars together, keeps a substantial slice for itself, and delivers the balance to whomever guessed all the right numbers.

As you can understand, the key of all this operation resides in the random drawing of the numbers. On one side is the state that tries to make the whole thing the most impartial. In Florida, pneumatic machines (always operated by gorgeous girls) and ping-pong balls are used. On the other side are all the players who try to influence the outcome of the numbers by using the most strange superstitions. There are people in fact who swear to have seen a bank president in a dark three-piece suit wearing a rabbit's foot necklace while watching the drawing on TV, and others who saw a nun making funny signals with the fingers of one hand, holding two black cats on a leash with the other!

When I was young in Italy, they did not use machines for the drawing, but did it by hand, blindfolding a girl (why always a girl?) and having her pick the numbers from the bottom of a sack. The custom was for the girl to be a virgin, and at the beginning there was no problem; except that, year after year the age of the girl had to be lowered until they realized that they could not find a virgin old enough to perform the task! That custom then was set aside.

Once the various states realized that Lotto involved big revenues they kept adding variations to the basic game of picking out the weekly numbers. Now if you want, you can play three, four, or five numbers every day. You can even scratch one-dollar tickets for an immediate winning up to $500. Kids scratch and sniff the perfume of candy; we scratch and hope to smell the perfume of money!

As it happens in any situation where money is involved, there is always someone who tries to beat illegally the system with all kind of tricks. That's why there is a very strict security involved in the organization of the game, the extraction of the numbers, and the payment of winnings. Even in the TV studio, invisible to the public, there are always a couple of security officers watching carefully the gorgeous girl extracting the numbers.

A BRIEF HISTORY
OF THE GAME

When Lotto was introduced for the first time in America, it was accepted with a certain amount of skepticism. But then the good old national love for gambling prevailed, and today the same people realize that they were wrong, especially after seeing the weekly amount of prizes and hearing others discuss the game and talk about what they would do with the money if they were the winners.

Let's forget then the nonbelievers and write instead for the majority—the believers—in line at the Lotto machine.

Lotto is a very old game. The term "lotto" itself seems to derive from the Teutonic word *hleut,* which became *hlot* in Middle and Old English. From this word then derived all the various European terms, the English "lottery," the Italian *lotto* and *lotteria,* the French *loterie,* and the Spanish *loteria.* We can find references to lotteries in the New and Old Testaments, where we learn that the first king of Israel was chosen by lot.

Historically, games linked to numbers can be traced back before the times of Assyria and Babylonia. Archaeologists found that one of the prehistoric tools used to play with numbers was a bone called *astragalus* also known as "heel bone." This bone has six sides and can be tossed like a die. In Ancient Egypt human *astragali* were used, but later were substituted with bones from sheep or goats. Since that time, players have been trying to break the mystery that surrounds the numbers and their chance to be picked as the winning ones.

Scientists of those times—really astrologer/magicians—thought it was possible to solve the mystery by studying the position of the planets and the moon in relationship to the month and the day of the year, or by the help of special esoteric doctrines linked to the Jewish Cabala.

While these doctrines were in the hands of a few scholars, less cultured people thought that the mystery of the numbers could be solved with a tool common to everybody but equally intriguing: the nightly dreams.

From the very beginning, people were fascinated by dreams, believed they could reveal hidden truths, and that their interpretation could help understand what was happening in the present and plan for the future.

Maybe the gods themselves were speaking to people in their sleep. Dreams became the object of study by priests of ancient religions and by experts who dedicated their lives to make a science out of this matter.

These experts, inspired by the Cabala and by numerology, tried to translate the symbols of dreams into numbers, thinking that the rigid laws of mathematics could help them find an answer to their questions.

The Greeks and Romans had their own lotteries but the Romans also had the habit, in the occasion of special dinners, to draw prizes amongst the guests. The first lottery in France was introduced in 1540 and in England in 1566, and from there passed to Colonial America. The lotteries had always been a good revenue for governments, that's why practically all the countries have one.

In Europe and in some parts of the United States, the most famous is the Irish Lottery, first for its high stakes and also because it is legal only in Ireland. The tickets must be smuggled out of the country, while the receipt must be smuggled in, and the whole operation acquires the charm characteristic of the forbidden things.

In Italy the game of Lotto was inherited from the Romans, therefore the tradition is ancient and wide-spread. In one place, however, people became especially involved in the game. In Naples, when the city did not yet belong to the kingdom of Italy, but was part of an independent country in the southern part of the peninsula called the Kingdom of the Two Sicilies, the game became so popular that even today the city can be called the "World Capital" of the game. This is the reason why, once I decided to write this book, I spent time there. The confusion of this city is unbelievable, and every time you cross the street your life is at stake because of the chaotic traffic. However, the Neapolitans are among the most good-natured and kind people in the world.

THE IMPORTANCE OF THE *PORTAFORTUNA* (TALISMAN)

While I was in Naples, besides the usual excursions to Capri, Ischia, Sorrento, and Positano, the places that must be visited by every good tourist, I often walked downtown. Looking at the store windows, which are a good mirror of the taste and the customs of the inhabitants of a city, I noticed something different from the other places I visited. In particular all the jewelers displayed huge sections of lucky charms of various sizes. All jewelers everywhere keep some of these gadgets, but here in Naples they had three or four times what I would have considered a normal amount. The same thing could be said for the stores selling custom jewelry.

Most of these charms represented four main symbols: first, *il corno,* "the horn," an ox's horn usually reproduced in red coral and mounted in gold. Second, *le corna,* "the horns," the reproduction of a closed fist with the index and the little finger up. Besides the function of bringing luck or keeping away the evil eye, it sometimes involves a judgement on the fidelity (or better, the infidelity) of a spouse. It could represent the word *cornuto* which can be translated in English to "cuckold" (which is also the favorite nickname given to the soccer umpires by discontented fans). The third lucky charm is the "hunchback," a miniature man with a big hump on his back. Rubbing the hump is supposed to bring the best of luck. The fourth is the number thirteen. Many people believe that this is a lucky number, but many others instead are afraid of it—so much so that in a lot of buildings the thirteenth floor does not exist. There is also a special word of Greek derivation to define the fear of number thirteen: *triskaidekaphobia.* These symbols can be found also as key-holders or even in the designs of ties and scarfs.

When I asked a Neapolitan friend the reason for this abundance of lucky charms, he told me nobody there would ever dare to go through life without a good *portafortuna,* or talisman. He explained that everyone had to find his own, usually an object as the horn or something similar. Otherwise how could you expect, for example, to win the Lotto game or to have any other strike of luck? As for himself, besides the little red horn hanging from a chain around his neck, he had his own routine. Every morning, getting out from home, he would stop at the coffee bar at the corner for a *cappuccino* with a *brioche.* Outside the bar there was a hunchback, who, for a few lire, would let customers rub his hump.

My friend said that he has been doing that for years and everything went well for him, except one week when the hunchback was in the hospital, he could not rub his back and somebody stole his wallet. I don't know if this story is true or not, but the fact that most gamblers or even simple card players are superstitious, is indisputable.

MEETING WITH THE
DREAM INTERPRETER

Maybe priests of ancient religions and experts in Cabala and numerology don't exist anymore in Naples, but they have been replaced by professional dream interpreters to whom people go with special or unusual dreams. Upon payment of a modest fee these experts decipher the dream and suggest the numbers to be played.

During my trip to Naples I searched for one of these interesting characters. After contacting a few of the local people, I finally met Gennaro Esposito, supposedly one of the best known local experts on interpreting dreams and figuring out numbers.

Gennaro lives in a crowded section of the city, in a small but neat apartment. The walls of his dining room (which doubles as his office), are covered with written testimonials of people that at one time or another won at the game. From the adjoining room, presumably the kitchen, comes an aroma of garlicky tomato sauce, the famous Neapolitan *pummarola*. At the time of my visit, my first thought was that if his performance on the job was as good as the smell of his sauce, his popularity was no surprise.

I had called for an appointment, but I didn't specify what I wanted from him. He was always very kind, but when I told him that I wanted to research and write on the interpretation of dreams and lotto numbers, I felt a little chill between us which lasted a few seconds. I could tell he was annoyed. He tried hard to speak Italian, but he couldn't help but go back often to a strong dialect, which at times was difficult to understand. From the way he was dressed, I could tell he wasn't making much money, but probably his popularity in certain strata of the population was a big enough reward for him. I wouldn't have been surprised if some of his clients paid him with a dozen eggs or a live goose, as I saw people doing in the Philippines, to the local faith-healers.

THEORIES ON DREAMS AND NUMBERS

Gennaro is a simple man, a bit shy too, but he makes an effort to explain in the best way he can his theories on dreams and numbers. This is the way he figures out dreams: first he divides them in several categories.

They can be triggered by something specific, or they can be completely spontaneous. Some dreams are definitely caused by the daily events of life—you may meet a friend today and dream at night of him or of something that is associated with him.

Or you may have eaten something too heavy for your digestion and you will have a nightmare. Or if tomorrow you have a job interview, tonight you'll go to bed very anxious and as a result you'll have a bad dream.

On the other hand, after a normal day you may dream many things that apparently have no reference to your everyday life and look like they came out of nowhere.

Dreams can adhere to reality or be totally unreal. They can show situations that can really happen (like eating or strolling in the park). Or they can show fantastic situations that in real life will never happen (like having wings like an angel and flying).

Dreams can be static or dynamic: you may stand still in a forest looking at the trees and the squirrels; or you may be doing something like crossing a river or travelling by train from one city to another.

Dreams can be made of a single image like the ocean, the mountains, a rainbow; or made out of a sequence of events such as going to the beach, seeing a man drowning, and then jumping in the water to save his life.

Gennaro says that no matter what the dream is, the most important (and, I add, complicated) thing to do is to isolate what he calls the "main spots" i.e. the thing (or the things) that are most valuable to you in the dream. Therefore you must analyze (not in psychoanalytical terms, please) the dream and find these "spots."

The fact is that very seldom dreams are made of one single thing like a dog or an airplane. Dreams are more like movies and the challenge is to put the elements of the dream together in a sequence.

For instance, you dream that you are at the theater with your family watching an opera, when you see two birds flying from one side to the other in front of the stage. You have to find out (and only you can do this) what is the most important thing for you: the theater, the family, the opera, or the birds.

Also very important is any number that comes out clearly in the dream. Think about the Number 2 of the two birds. Or if you dream about a young woman and she tells you that she is 24 years old, that number is

very important and could be one of the numbers to be played. This seems obvious but
many times the strange facts happening in the
dream take your attention away from the
simplest things like single numbers.

"Once we have determined the 'spots' of
the dream, how do we find out the numbers
to play?" I asked Gennaro.

"That is the simplest thing," he answered.
"Just look at this." Then he handed me a
piece of paper with some letters and some
numbers arranged in the following manner:

4	3	2	1	9	8	7	6	5
A	B	C	D	E	F	G	H	I
J	K	L	M	N	O	P	Q	R
S	T	U	V	W	X	Y	Z	

To each letter of the alphabet corresponds
a number and if you are able to read and add
numbers, you can use this schedule.

Take the dream at the theater for example. You have:

T 3	F 8	O 8	F 8	S 4
H 6	A 4	P 7	L 2	T 3
E 9	M 1	E 9	Y 7	A 4
A 4	I 5	R 5	I 5	G 7
T 3	L 2	A 4	N 9	E 9
E 9	Y 7	——	G 7	——
R 9	——	33		27
——	27		B 3	
43			I 5	
			R 5	
			D 1	
			S 4	
			——	
			56	

The sum of the value of the letters of FLYING BIRDS is 56, but if where you play Lotto the numbers don't go this high, you add the two figures 5 and 6, to find the number to be played: 11.

At this point I tried to interrupt him and asked, "Gennaro, don't you think this thing about letters and numbers is a little too simple? Why do the numbers go 4-3-2-1-9-8-7-6-5 and not 1-2-3-etc. like they should?" Gennaro looked at me in a funny way and asked me if I was trying to teach him his own business. "Don't you know," he said, "that I learned all this from a centuries-old tradition?"

Then, he continued, there are a few other things to consider: one is the influence of the moon on the dreams and then there are the days and the months of the dreams.

Starting from the first day of the new moon, keep in mind that whatever you dream on the 1st, 4th, 8th, 10th, 12th, 13th, 16th, 27th, and 29th day, has a very good chance of becoming true and should be considered a good omen. However, whatever you dream on the 6th, 19th, 22nd, 26th and 28th day, has a bad connotation. Don't tell anybody what you dream the 7th and 14th day. The other days are of no special meaning.

The numbers for each day of the week are:

Sunday	8
Monday	11
Tuesday	9
Wednesday	3
Thursday	18
Friday	21
Saturday	7

The numbers for the months are:

January	13
February	5
March	4
April	3
May	12
June	8
July	25
August	1
September	7
October	9
November	6
December	12

Some people give importance to the number of the astrological sign of the dreamer:

Aries	10
Taurus	8
Gemini	39
Cancer	11
Leo	12
Virgo	3
Libra	7
Scorpio	16
Sagittarius	1
Capricorn	30
Aquarius	17
Pisces	10

There is a rule also on how long to play a set of numbers, and that is for a maximum of 177 days (about 25 weeks) after the night of the dream.

When Gennaro finished his explanation and I realized the large amount of numbers one has to reckon with, I was really angry with him.

"Are you pulling my leg? How can you say that picking numbers is so simple?" I almost yelled at him.

He answered, "It is simple once you know how, but do you expect to wake up each Monday morning and go get the millions you won the week before? Selecting numbers to play is like any other human activity; it requires training and experience. So you have to start playing and modify your technique according to the results."

CONSIDERATIONS ON THE SYSTEM

It is likely that to many people this relationship between dreams and numbers could seem totally nonexistent, but before dismissing the whole thing as a lot of hogwash, let's make a few considerations.

According to some researchers, through our dreams we have access to a dimension common to every person, sometimes called the collective unconscious. They say that this dimension is out of our usual concept of time, so there is no past, no future—just an everlasting present where whatever happens, happened, or will happen, coexist.

If we accept this theory as true, once we reach this dimension, we may get the knowledge of facts yet to happen, like which numbers will be picked in the next draw.

Unfortunately our personal unconscious has the bad habit of using symbols to deliver the information through our dreams. Therefore, in order to understand these symbols, most of the time we need the help of a psychoanalyst, a witch doctor, a shaman, or a Neapolitan dream interpreter, according to the culture we belong.

Another theory affirms that all humans have some extrasensory powers, more or less developed, that enable them to foresee facts that will happen in the future. Some will do that in a state of trance, but the majority will need the help of an object or an action that will vary from person to person.

For example: some will read the palm of a hand (chiromancy or palmistry); some a deck of cards (Tarot); some, like the ancient Romans, will interpret the flying of birds (or nithomancy); some will look at the tea leaves or the coffee grounds left at the bottom of a cup; some at the dropping of animals (scatomancy); and some will rely on the interpretation of dreams (onyromancy), as it is the case of Gennaro, and as we have read even in the Bible.

My recommendation is that if you ever go to Naples, look up Gennaro, who is listed in the telephone book. You will have a very interesting experience. He told me that when he has to deal with English-speaking people, he calls his cousin Salvatore, who lived for five years in Brooklyn, to act as the official interpreter.

Besides advising the numbers to play, Gennaro Esposito is the recipient of a popular tradition, passed orally from generation to generation through the centuries: the prediction of the future through the meaning of dreams. After all, whatever we dream has its origin in our unconscious mind and, even if the relationship with our everyday life may not be immediately clear, somehow it is related with our personality, and potentially it may contain the seed of development of our future life. The dictionary which follows has been suggested by Gennaro, but before giving it to me he insisted that he was only reporting what he learned himself, without adding anything. As you will see, the concepts are simple and represent the typical environment and feelings of a person, with an accent on family, love, and money which usually are the most important features in an average life. He also stressed that he gave me only a very general interpretations of the objects and the situations.

USING THE DICTIONARY OF DREAMS

As you may understand, it is impossible to define every single thing you may dream, so it is up to you to refer to the closest possible concept. If you dream a slipper or a boot, evidently you have to refer to the term "shoes." The same applies to modern terms that were unknown not only to the cabalists but also to the more recent folk tradition.

As far as the specific use of the dictionary, Gennaro gave me these suggestions which I will explain with an example. Suppose you dream of a dancing, black cat. For the interpretation of the future, you have to consult the following terms in the dictionary: first about the subject (the cat); second about the adjective (black); and third about the action (to dance). It is then up to you to put together the message of the dream with the help of your unconscious mind, which will hold your attention on the meaningful particulars of the dream.

If I had to interpret this dream for myself, I could say that "people who spread lies about me" (the cat), and "who make me sad and withdrawn" (black), will be cancelled and replaced by something else which will make my life lucky and happy" (the dance).

The numbers to be played in this case would be 2, 32, and 66 for the cat; 11, 20, and 29 for the color black; and 7 and 46 for the dance. If these numbers are too many to be played, take some out starting from the end; for example, cancel first the 66 for the cat and the 29 for the color black, and so on.

Before you start trying this method and this dictionary, let me give you some personal advice.

First, while you shouldn't take this book too lightly, don't go to the other extreme and wrap it in a silk cloth like certain Tarot readers do with their deck of cards. Just keep it under your pillow and don't lend it to anybody.

Keep in mind that even though much of this knowledge has been passed orally from generation to generation, it still plays an important role in the life of people, much as folk medicine does.

Secondly: don't take Lotto too seriously; remember it is only a game. If you want to play the numbers, do it with an amount of money that does not disrupt your life to the point it creates financial problems for your family.

SUPPOSE THAT YOU PLAY AND WIN...

Finally all my problem will be solved, you will say.

Hold on one minute! I am sure that you can handle $200,000 or $300,000. But do you have the financial mind to handle $7 or $8 million? Yes, I know, you can hire an expert to help you, but can you trust him? Are you sure that your tax man will save you enough money? What about your stock broker: maybe he'll start playing around with your money. You can invest in real estate or gold, but what will happen if the market goes down? You may risk spending sleepless nights on that cruise you could finally afford!

OK, I am only kidding! I know what you think: first let me win the Lotto, then I'll think about all the problems. This is the common attitude and probably also the best. But the fact still remains that everybody is comfortable at a different financial level and has different feelings toward money. One may be best at living with three kids on $25,000 or $30,000 a year, but when he finds himself from morning to night with an income ten times larger, he may really be in serious trouble. The pressure becomes strong, everyone is asking for money—from his own relatives to 500 different charities. He may feel guilty if he does not share his own good luck. But who is really in need? To whom must he give precedence?

Personally I know of two cases, one in the United States and one in Italy, where the winners reacted in a strange way. In New York State, a blue-collar worker who won a large amount of money tried at the beginning not to change his life and remained working, maintaining his usual lifestyle. A few days later, when the news of his winning became public, he was so criticized and ridiculed, that in order to get a little peace, he moved out of state.

In Monza, Italy, a town close to Milano, a priest was playing the equivalent of a dollar every week, on the five numbers of the Italian Lotto Game. He had good intentions, in case that three or four numbers came out, to spend some money for his parish and give the rest to the Church in Rome. To guess all the numbers was so far from his mind, that he did not even take it into consideration. But one week, that's just what happened. He guessed the whole *cinquina,* all five numbers, and the pay-off was extremely high. This poor fellow, who was a priest but also a simple man, found himself divided between the greed for all this money and the duties of his mission. In short, he lost his head and had to be confined in an asylum.

DICTIONARY
OF
DREAMS

ACTIONS AND FEELINGS

Abort
Accumulate

Be jealous
Beg
Bleed
Breast-feed
Build
Buy

Call
Commit
  suicide
Cross
Cry

Dance
Dig
Drink
Drive

Eat
Envy
Escort

Fall
Flee
Forgive

Get angry
Get drunk
Get married
Get sick
Get wet

Hug
Hurt

Inherit

Jump

Kill
Kiss
Knock

Laugh
Leave
Lead
Lock

Lose
Love
Lust

Paint
Pay
Play
Perform
Pray

Sail
Sell
Shave
Shoot
Sing
Sleep
Smell
Smoke
Sweat
Swim

Travel

Walk

Psychologists say that dreams are like a safety valve through which man gets rid of some of the stress stored during the day.

The meaning of a dream is never due to chance but hides the effort of each person to reveal the problems of the soul. That's why the actions and the feelings appearing in the dream are so important.

If rightly interpreted, they indicate the true desires, fears, and lusts of the unconscious.

ABORT [9 13]

- Means suffering.

- Social life is a failure.

- Only if the abortion is natural, it means the end of all troubles.

ACCUMULATE [15 45]

- It's the symbol of avarice and egotism.

- In our dreams it is always a bad omen.

- If you accumulate money and precious objects, it means you will be losing whatever is dearest to you.

BE JEALOUS [10 49]

- Insecurity leading to depression.

- You are often ready for a fight within the family and outside.

- The only way out is through showing your true good feelings.

BEG [12 37]

- Happiness is here and so is the will to make others happy.

- If you dream to give money to a beggar, you will be very lucky and unexpected success will be with you shortly.

BLEED [16 27]

- Be careful about unfaithful friends. They try to ruin your career.

- Your health may be also in danger; not so much your physical health but mainly your emotions.

BREAST-FEED [2 3 42]

- Affection.

- If a woman breast-feeds, it means that she has a noble soul and lucky will be the man that will live with her.

- If you watch breast-feeding, it means you are lacking affection. Try to show your virtues and you will not be alone for long.

- If a man has this dream, he is misunderstood in his family and will suffer deeply.

BUILD [30 33]

- Building or having a palace built means you will have a long, satisfying life.

- If you build something with which you are not satisfied, you must expect a very bad period in your finances.

BUY [14 50]

- Means fulfillment of your desires. The amount of things you can buy in a dream or in real life is practically infinite. Here are a few examples, but in general, we refer to the specific item dreamed:

- To buy meat means that your income will soon be growing.

- To buy fish means that your health is getting better and better.

- To buy flowers means that your love life is improving.

- To buy fruit is no good for your finances.

CALL [3 61]

- To call somebody in a dream means you are missing some of the qualities that person has and that you admire the most.

- To hear your name called by strangers means that soon you will need help and a stranger will give you assistance.

- If you are called by somebody you know, this person soon will fall sick and perhaps will die.

- To be called by a dead person is being warned against some physical or economic danger.

COMMIT SUICIDE [9 65]

- Misfortune is hitting you.

- Maybe you are the cause of your own troubles. Even if it is someone else's fault, it will be a long time before you are able to stand up again.

CROSS [17 38]

- To cross something is a symbol of security and curiosity.

- To cross a field means that a secret desire will be fulfilled.

- To cross a wood means that a secret love will be reciprocated.

- To cross a creek with clear water means that whatever you will try will succeed.

CRY [24 51]

- It shows nostalgic and lonely feelings.
- But you can be sure to receive good news or a valuable gift.
- Joy will fill your house.

DANCE [7 46]

- You enjoy the lighter aspects of life.
- The child hidden in you is having a great time.
- You may expect very good fortune.
- If you see other people dancing, the good fortune is limited to your business.

DIG [16 65]

- It's good to be stubborn.
- Keep asking. After many days during which nothing happens, your request will be answered. This goes for lovers and gamblers, too.

DRINK [18 22 64]

- It shows our desire to learn and evolve.

- It is positive because it means the dreamer wants to fight the negative aspects of his character.

- To drink good fresh water means success in business and in love.

- To drink liquor means a brief disease is ahead.

- To drink wine means you will spend some time with friends.

- To drink beer means troubles in family life.

- To drink coffee is good for business and love (almost like water).

- To drink milk is very good for all your financial enterprises.

DRIVE [3 20]

- To drive a carriage pulled by an animal signifies that something unusual, but good, will happen in your life.

- To drive a car means that you are looking for something, but with uncertain results.

- If you are driven in a car, you will find a lucky path in a difficult situation.

EAT [1 8 19]

- A great dream if you are a farmer—all your work will be rewarded.

- If you see other people eating, you may be too greedy. Try to moderate yourself.

- If you are eating, your career is blooming and all your efforts will be financially rewarded.

- If you don't like what you are eating, money will come to you, especially if you are a gambler.

ENVY [5 59]

- It is a sign of discontent and loneliness.

- Sometimes when you experience negative feelings like envy in real life they come out in dreams.

- It's not a good dream.

ESCORT [6 13]

- A woman dreaming to be escorted by a younger man shows a hidden insecurity that will surface in a romantic situation.

FALL [17 30]

- Lack of drive.

- You cannot immerse yourself in anything.

- You complain about bad luck, but it is all your fault.

- You don't commit yourself enough. This happens also in your romantic involvements.

FLEE [14 27 32]

- Fleeing in the face of danger means fear of success.

- Success will come anyway, but you will have to fight hard for it.

FORGIVE [4 21]

- Narrow-mindedness.

- If you forgive others, it means that in life you are dealing with dangerous people.

- If you are forgiven it means you lack personality.

- Listening to influential people can save you lots of problems.

GET ANGRY [14 33]

- Egotism and weak character.

- In real life you get frustrated by all the outrages you had to suffer and the dream is the only way to vent your repressed feelings and take revenge.

GET DRUNK [11 40]

- Luck and well being.

- All the worries and trouble of the past are over. It doesn't depend on you, but is due to a series of lucky events.

- This is good time for travels and for meeting people who later can be of help in your profession.

GET MARRIED [3 10 36]

- Dreaming of getting married for a man is a sign of inner strength.

- For a woman, it instead means fear of the future and the wish to get rid of a feeling of insecurity.

GET MARRIED [8 26]

- Infidelity and sadness.

- Married people are missing something in their union.

- Single and older people feel lonely.

- You may go on a trip that will be a waste of time.

GET SICK [8 43]

- Sadness.

- Very negative.

- If you are already sick in bed with an illness, your disease will worsen.

GET WET [46 47]

- Cold water means you will have trouble with a loved one and his or her family.

- Hot water means prosperity.

- In the ocean, means the good feelings you have toward others will be reciprocated.

- In the rain, means you will receive good news or will get a gift.

- In a pool or in a pond, better to wait some time, this is not a good moment for your projects.

HUG [15 31]

- If you hug somebody it indicates insecurity and you will not be very happy in love or in business.

- For a woman hugging a stranger means to accept advances by a man while being aware that she's putting herself in a dangerous situation.

HURT [4 23]

- When you dream that your body hurts, without any visible wound, you are afraid of facing reality. Most likely, when you wake up your first thought is to remain in bed and forget about the dangers outside.

INHERIT [16 53]

- It is not a good dream.

- It means that the dreamer tries to solve everyday problems with the help of others and not with his or her own strength.

- To inherit gold means to lose money.

JUMP [8 12 37]

- Instability.

- You may start something because you are certain that you will get help from others, only to realize at the last minute that you have been left alone.

- Don't get involved in a romantic relationship. After you fall in love the other person will laugh at you.

KILL [2 34]

- It is a bad dream.

- Many aggressive feelings hide in your unconscious.

- If you kill a woman, a period of great sadness is ahead of you.

- If you kill a man, somebody is plotting against you.

- If you kill animals you will be gravely offended.

- If you get killed, someone very close to you is trying to hurt you.

KISS [22 37]

- People you care for don't reciprocate your feelings.

- Loved ones are indifferent to your advances.

- Your efforts to be friendly are not acknowledged, even your family is not as close as it should be.

- In business, credit is becoming tight.

- Artists don't receive the praise they deserve.

- To change these trends, you must become less egotistical.

KNOCK [1 6 31]

- Your feelings have been hurt.

- Don't expect the door on which you knock to open. It very seldom does. But if the door opens, you will have a period of great happiness.

LAUGH [9 41]

- Even if you are not socially and culturally prominent, you are compensated by having a happy personality and a good mood.

- Whenever it looks like you have a problem, something will happen or someone will intervene to save the situation.

LEAVE [26 60]

- You want to get rid of all your worries and you will work hard to do it.

- At the end you will be rewarded with big financial gains.

LEAD [38 43]

- Dreaming to be the leader of an army may correspond to real life. Maybe you will be offered a job or responsibility. In this case, don't hesitate, you have all the qualities to succeed.

LOCK [13 59]

- If you are locked in a room and you try unsuccessfully to get out, it means people are pulling your leg and you feel rejected.

- If you try to enter a room through a locked door and you succeed, it means that your love is endangered by a rival but you are not scared. Through your self-confidence you will come out as a winner in this situation.

LOSE [5 62]

- All your sacrifice may be useless.

- The people around you are ungrateful.

- Parents will suffer for the behavior of their children.

- Work can make you overtired.

LOVE [42 55]

- The love you have for others means you are happy with your present situation.

- The love others have for you means that you will be free from the anxiety that you have experienced up to now.

- Any dream with love foretells a period of stability and good fortune.

LUST [8 30]

- Usually the dream of lust reflects the way you have been brought up and the kind of sexual education you received.

- Dreams of lust are believed to be the way you get rid of your repressed desires.

- They generally mean inhibition and are a bad omen.

PAINT [11 31]

- Symbol of the will to improve ourselves.

- Painting a portrait means that we will have the help of influential people.

PAY [6 47]

- The dream of paying someone with cash is not a good sign.

- Usually corresponds to a period of bad health or emotional draining.

- Postpone important decisions to a later date.

PERFORM (AS AN ACTOR) [27 34]

- Dreaming of being an actor means you will have to work hard for every project you have, but at the end success is sure.

- Seeing an actress on the stage means a very pleasant period of your life is ahead.

PLAY [2 5 64]

- If you dream of playing Lotto or roulette, always try to remember the numbers—they might be the winners in real life.

- Playing games as a child is a symbol of a simple soul with the tendency to be irresponsible.

- Playing casino games shows a very anxious personality.

- Playing cards with other players means that someone is trying to cheat you.

PRAY [10 39]

- You will come out very distressed from a dangerous situation.

- Keeping your loved one faithful to you will not be an easy task, but your stubbornness will overcome any obstacle.

SAIL [8 22]

- You want to get rid of all your worries and you are strong enough to succeed.

- This is always a good dream and brings good news and gains in the financial field.

SELL [21 67]

- You have the tendency to give more value to material pleasures than to spirituality.

- You are bored and dissatisfied.

- A period of anxiety and fear is ahead.

SHAVE [32 34]

- Shrewdness.

- You will overcome competition especially in love.

- Take better care of your body which is not in top shape due to job stress.

- There is the risk to be easygoing and someone could take advantage of you at work.

SHOOT [7 39]

- Shooting a firearm symbolizes repressed feelings. For your well-being, it is necessary to expose what is making you unhappy. It is the only way to regain peace.

SING [36 45]

- It is a symbol of good feelings and of desire to grow up spiritually.

- To sing in church means that you will be rewarded for your good actions.

- To sing in the street means that for a while your life will be happy and without serious problems.

SLEEP [19 63]

- It is a negative dream. You are withdrawing from your responsibilities because you think you are not capable of facing them.

- Your self-confidence is gone and so is your will to fight.

SMELL [5 21]

- If the odor is good or bad has no importance in the dream.

- It is important to foresee danger. It is essential not to be caught by surprise.

SMOKE [23 66]

- Disappointments, one after the other.

- You have to face a lot of troubles.

- To dream of smoking cigarettes inhibits your love life.

- Smoking a cigar brings losses in business.

- Smoking a pipe means your health is not in good shape.

SWEAT [13 49]

- A dream of sweating is not very common.

- It predicts a great success.

- If you have any doubt about a new venture, don't hesitate. Jump into it.

SWIM [24 51]

- Sooner or later you will have a nervous breakdown.

- You may run into a loss of money, fights with family members, or diseases that will leave you shocked for a short period. But with patience, everything will go back to normal.

TRAVEL [4 14 68]

- You are pushed toward a substantial change in your life, but whoever is pushing you does it for his or her interest and not for yours, as you are lead to believe.

- The situation is dangerous and in the best of instances, this change will be completely useless.

WALK [2 18 53]

- Being far from home.

- If you have lived always in the same place you grew up, life will take you far away.

- If you already left home, you will get very homesick.

- In business, you have to be aware that someone is trying to cheat you.

ANIMALS

Alligator
Ant

Bat
Bear
Bee
Beetle
Bird
Blackbird
Bug
Butterfly

Cat
Cock

Deer
Dog
Donkey
Dove

Eagle
Elephant

Fish
Fly
Fox

Horse

Lamb
Lizard

Monkey
Mosquito
Mouse

Owl
Ox

Pig
Porpoise

Ram
Rat

Scorpion
Shrimp
Snail
Snake
Spider
Swallow

Toad

Wolf

Animals were the first companions of man on earth. He learned almost immediately that he could use some as food or help in his daily work, but he also discovered that he had to fear many others always ready to take his life.

Therefore, according to their meekness or their ferocity, popular belief considered animals as a bad or good omen.

The ancient Romans used to foretell the outcome of certain events by watching the flight of the birds.

ALLIGATOR [5 44]

- A mean atmosphere surrounds you.

- False friends envy your status and would like to see you return to poverty.

- An alligator in muddy waters with blood around it is one of the worst dreams, and forecasts some action that could land you in jail.

ANT [13 23]

- Ants are symbols of hard labor and if you work hard like them, you will get the best rewards.

- The future from a financial point of view will be much brighter.

BAT [8 55]

- Due to the popular belief, this poor harmless animal has a very bad reputation.

- Dreaming of a bat foretells bad luck and disease. If you should dream of a bat inside the house, you can expect a lot of gossip about you.

BEAR [23 60]

- Generally speaking, this animal is not a good omen.

- It means your friends are not sincere.

- If you kill the bear though, it means you will prevail over your foe.

- If you follow the bear, it means you will complete your projects in the best way.

BEE [11 19 47]

- It is a symbol of sweetness and energy.

- If you dream of a flying bee, it means you are a person of high spiritual feelings and people will enjoy your company.

- If you kill a bee some of your projects will go wrong.

- If you are stung by a bee, you will experience a short period of worries.

BEETLE [4 31]

- It is a symbol of transformation.

- You are drawn toward meditation and spirituality.

- Your life is going to proceed smoothly for a substantial period of time.

BIRD [11 43 47 64]

- This animal can be a bad or a good omen according to the way you dream of it.

- If you see birds flying toward the east everything will go smoothly for you; but birds flying toward the west means there will be many obstacles in your life.

- Birds flying high brings good luck to you, but if they fly low, close to the ground, be very careful in all your enterprises.

- To hear birds singing means good health. If at the moment you are sick, your illness will be very short.

- Feeding the birds means monetary gains.

BLACKBIRD [19 52]

- A special bird, maybe due to its color.

- Dreaming of it means somebody is gossiping about you.

- You have to act immediately if you want to restore your good reputation.

BUG [2 18]

- Your life is becoming more complicated every day.

- People around you, especially members of your family, are very careless, and you don't have enough time to remedy their mistakes.

- You may get sick for a short period.

BUTTERFLY [17 24]

- It is a symbol of kindness.

- If you dream of a butterfly on a flower it means that your soul, after many worries, will find a period of peace.

- If you catch a butterfly, it means that in your romantic life you have unsteady feelings.

CAT [2 32 66]

- Brings treason and deception.

- Don't trust the people around you.

- Somebody is trying to spread lies about you and may write anonymous letters.

- If you leave the house for a trip be sure that all the locks are in working order, because thieves will try to get in.

COCK [13 34]

- It means prosperity and power.

- In a very short time you will complete a project that is still an idea in your mind.

- Fiancés will get married sooner than they thought, thanks to some unexpected financial help.

- People who went through surgery can be sure of good results of the operation.

DEER [16 56]

- It is the symbol of victory of good over evil.

- If you dream of a running deer, it means that all your doubts will disappear.

- If you kill a deer, it means that your enemies are trying to put a lot of obstacles in front of you.

DOG [18 29]

- If you dream of petting a nice dog, you tend to be altruistic and luck will be with you.

- On the contrary, a snarling dog means that you are selfish and egotistical and it is time for you to change your attitude.

- A barking dog is a danger for married people; it is a warning against temptation.

- A hunting dog means strength and self-assurance.

- If the dog is white, it brings very good luck.

DONKEY [5 40 63]

- It is a symbol of mediocrity.

- You did not work hard enough in the past and now you have to face the consequences.

- If you ride a donkey, it means that you are trying to make up now for past errors. It will not be easy, but with a big effort you may again be proud of yourself.

DOVE [10 42]

- Naiveté may be considered a virtue, but too much of it can become stupidity.

- You are too fair and somebody could take advantage of you.

- You may be considered responsible for something that you never did.

- Single women beware of easy promises of marriage.

EAGLE [19 42 47]

- Strength, intelligence, and eagerness to win.

- An eagle flying high in the sky means that your present status will improve in the near future.

- A rapacious and ferocious eagle means you will get a short but serious disease.

- Do your best not to dream a dead eagle because that is the end of all your hopes.

ELEPHANT [1 22]

- You want to emerge.

- You will receive soon an executive's duty.

- A married woman who dreams of an elephant should take over the direction of the family because her husband is weak and does not know how to handle the budget and the education of the children.

FISH [30 61]

- It is a symbol of luck, spiritual strength, and fertility.

- If you catch some fish, most of your wishes will come true.

- If you see fish swimming at the surface, business and love will receive a boost; you may get married very soon.

- If you see dead fish in the water, your status will stand still and no improvement is in sight.

FLY [8 69]

- It means lots of troubles and worries; nothing serious but enough to make you uncomfortable.

- If you are bothered by buzzing flies, it means that friends and relatives are envious of you and they try to make things difficult for you.

FOX [3 27 34]

- You are honest and sincere in your feelings, and you think that people are like you. Unfortunately this is not true and soon enough you will realize that being naive does not help you a bit.

- Plenty of troubles are ahead.

- To kill a fox means you will find out who is slandering you.

HORSE [7 55]

- The meaning of the dream depends on the image of the horse.

- A black horse for a single man means a marriage to a beautiful woman with a very bad temper; for a single woman, it means a happy marriage with a rich man.

- A herd of white horses is a symbol of beauty and virtue. For singles it means a happy marriage; for married people, a happy family life.

LAMB [5 15]

- Friendship and peace.

- You are well respected in your work environment.

- There will not be anything amazing in your future, but it will be bright and serene.

- There is a big buy in the immediate future. It could be a house, a car, or a jewel.

- Trust the advice of a close friend.

- For lovers, all the past quarrels are gone; happy days are ahead.

LIZARD [31 55]

- It means guilty feelings, indecision, and need of protection.

- To dream of a lizard on a wall, resting in the sun, means you don't know how to start facing your problems.

MONKEY [3 14 64]

- A very bad dream for lovers.

- Envious people are ready to gossip and in

general, to make life hard for you. You have to be very private and avoid showing your feelings.

- Problems at work have to be solved without anyone's help.

- Very few of your friends can be trusted.

MOSQUITO [2 34]

- One person is trying to ridicule your behavior. Find out who this person is and keep him or her at a distance.

- If you are preparing a picnic or short trip, you must not let anybody join you at the last minute. This person may disrupt all your plans and ruin your little vacation.

MOUSE [27 29]

- It is a symbol of shame and fraud.

- Your success is not due to your personal talent, but to deception.

- Someone will uncover your actions and you will realize that a more honest behavior would have given you less success but more appreciation.

- If you don't feel well, do not hide anything from the doctor, otherwise you will
  make his task too difficult.

OWL [5 13 17]

- To dream of an owl is absolutely a no-no.

- Everything is in danger: business, love,
  and health.

- Bad luck will not hit you directly, but will
  surely hit somebody close to you.

- Just float through life until everything
  blows over.

OX [10 22 48]

- You will experience slow but sure progress in all fields of your life.

- All your past efforts are rewarded.

- If you dream of two oxen pulling a cart, it
  means that somebody will join you in
  your activities, maybe a partner, or even a
  spouse, if you are single.

PIG [19 46]

- Is a symbol of sexuality, but also of fraud.

- If you dream of pigs that eat, it means that your sexual desires are very strong, even if you don't want to admit them, and you tend to satisfy them in every way.

- Be careful not to be obsessed by sex: other aspects of life are of equal, if not bigger, importance.

PORPOISE [32 50]

- A porpoise is a symbol of spiritual renewal, and has almost religious connotations.

- To ride a porpoise means that you have overcome your interior doubts.

- To dream of a porpoise that follows you means that you are looking for protection and advice.

RAM [30 68]

- To see a grazing ram means that you can count on your friends for help.

- If the ram is running after you, it indicates danger, but also that you have the qualities and the strength to defend yourself.

RAT [17 35]

- To dream of rats means quarrels with your partners or neighbors.

- If you catch a rat, you outwit your enemies.

- If you kill a rat, you may win a contest, but the prize will not be of much value.

SCORPION [20 42]

- To dream of a scorpion means fear.

- Don't trust anybody, especially your dearest friends. If a scorpion bites you, it is too late to be careful, they have already harmed you.

- Privacy is the best defense.

SHRIMP [13 43]

- Everybody around wants something from you. They may ask for it openly or they may try not to reveal their intentions.

- If you eat the shrimp, you are aware of what to expect from them and you know how to avoid their pressure.

- If you see dead shrimp at the market, watch that your loved one is on the verge of cheating on you.

SNAIL [8 16 46]

- You tend to be shy and lazy.

- You are not living a full life. If you don't do something about it, you will sink into mediocrity and miss the most interesting aspects of the world.

SNAKE [47 22]

- One interpretation of this dream is that you are surrounded by danger but that you can defend yourself with success.

- Only if the snake coils around you does it mean that you are powerless against this danger.

- The other interpretation is explicitly sexual: for a woman it could mean the fear of a sexual encounter due to poor education on the matter; for both men and women, it could mean the surfacing of homosexual tendencies.

SPIDER [18 23 36]

- Victory is with you.

- If you are an artist, success is yours.

- Single women will meet interesting men, but marriage is not necessarily to follow.

- Men may receive an honorary appointment, not financially rewarding, but important for their social lives.

SWALLOW [19 35]

- A very good dream for the family life.

- If the swallow is flying over you, everything is running smoothly and even bitter, unavoidable fights with your spouse are resolved completely.

- If you see swallows migrate, you will receive bad news.

TOAD [6 28 31]

- This animal is closely linked to witchcraft. To dream of it may indicate wickedness directed against you.

- You aren't strong enough to defend yourself alone. You may need the help of someone who is familiar with black magic.

WOLF [10 18]

- It is the symbol of light prevailing over dark, good over evil.

- It means strength and courage.

- To capture a wolf means to be able to face all situations, including the most physically dangerous.

- If a woman dreams of being attacked by a wolf, it shows her fear of being romantically involved.

COLORS

Black
Blue
Brown

Green
Gray

Orange

Pink
Purple

Red

White

Yellow

If you think that your dreams are in black and white, psychologists say it is not true.

The fact is that you have the tendency to forget the colors because you give more weight to the characters and the actions of the dream.

But if you can remember them, be aware that the colors are very important.

Pale and fading colors mean your mind is calm and peaceful; dark and contrasting ones instead denote an agitated and violent soul.

BLACK [11 20 29]

- Means mourning, death, withdrawal, and all that is negative.
- Dreaming black is a bad omen. You may be in a phase of pessimism and you can see only the worst side of life.

BLUE [13 8 21]

- Spirituality and peace.
- Can be associated with the sky, the ocean, and with infinity.
- It shows a peaceful soul that aims toward meditation, idealism, and romanticism.

BROWN [27 25]

- Is associated with the earth and means security, tranquillity, and reflectivity.
- The soul of the dreamer tends toward sweetness and virtue.

GREEN [31 26 6]

- It is a very good color.
- Hope and confidence.

- Your health is good, your spirit is serene and joyful.

- Great things lie in front of you, but if the green is very dark, it could mean envy and slander.

GRAY [28 18 43]

- Shows sadness and loneliness.

- It means introversion and the difficulty of communicating with others.

- You know you are not fully understood and this makes you unhappy.

ORANGE [33 30 6]

- Encompasses the hot passion of red and the confidence of yellow.

- Always has a good meaning.

- Foretells cheerfulness and happy love.

PINK [23 44]

- Means happiness.

- Is a color favorable to engaged couples.

- A problem that delays the marriage, like

finding a place to live or a job, is going to be solved soon in the best way.

PURPLE [34 2]

- The near future is not favorable.

- You may be suddenly separated from a loved one.

- Could be the death of a relative or the parting from a lover.

- Happiness is still far away.

RED [17 7]

- Is the color of violence and aggressiveness, but also of deep love.

- Married people will fight for a while; lovers instead will be united by violent passion.

- If you are looking for a job, you will find it soon, but it will hide some danger.

WHITE [29 24 18]

- Only if it is the purest white does it mean honesty and integrity.

- But every little stain is a gossip about you.

- Don't trust even your best friends, they may lie to you.

YELLOW [29 27 9]

- Jealousy.

- People say something bad about your loved one and you will have the tendency to believe them, but they are lying because they are envious.

- If you are looking for a job, it will take a while to find the right one.

PERSONS

Actor
Admiral
Angel

Barber
Beggar
Blind person
Brother
Bus driver
Butcher

Carpenter
Clown
Creditor

Daughter
Dead person
Devil
Doctor
Dwarf

Farmer
Father
Friend

Ghost
Giant
Gypsy

Hairdresser
Hermit
Horseman
Humpback

Judge

King

Lover
 (woman)
Lover (man)
Lawyer

Maid
Mail carrier
Mother

Nun
Nurse

Old man
Old woman

Pilot
Policeman
Priest

Queen

Sister
Soldier
Son

Teacher
Thief

When dreaming, you usually have the main role in the dream, but you may not look like you do in reality.

Sometimes you see yourself as younger or older, or even looking like a total stranger. You may be engaged in doing something very unusual or you may find yourself in company of unknown people.

It is through the study of these symbols that is possible for you to understand your own personality.

ACTOR [7 35]

- This dream means incapability of adapting to reality.

- It is a symbol of fraud and corruption.

- An actor performing a drama on the stage means that the fraud is coming from people that you have been trusting.

ADMIRAL [11 43]

- It is a very good omen.

- You will become more important socially because of an award.

- The more the admiral is dressed up, and the more medals he has, the more happy and cheerful you will be.

ANGEL [4 21 36]

- Dreaming of an angel means good news will be coming soon.

- Somebody is protecting you and this gives you security and peace.

- If an angel talks to you, it means your good qualities will be recognized.

- An angel talking to you in church means your behavior often has been reproachable and it is necessary for you to be more careful in the way you deal with people.

- Only if you dream of a falling angel does the dream become dangerous, and no matter how you behave, it will be very hard for you to be on good terms with the people around you.

BARBER [10 38]

- Gossips and fraud.

- If the barber is shaving you, it means annoying delays in business.

- If the barber is cutting your hair, be aware that soon somebody will try to rip you off.

BEGGAR [6 44]

- Envy, narrow-mindedness, and stinginess.

- It means defeat and surrender.

- Only if you dream of giving something to the beggar does it mean you are aware of what is going on and you try to fight back.

BLIND PERSON [6 15]

- The meaning of this dream is very similar to the one about the beggar.

- Luck is slipping away from you because you cannot spot the chances of improvement you meet in your life.

- Try not to dream of a blind beggar. If you do, it means you are totally lost in a situation that could lead to a serious depression.

BROTHER [3 24]

- If you dream of your brother or brothers as happy and wealthy people, soon you will have many reasons to rejoice.

- Dreaming of them as unhappy and poor will reflect your own situation, not as much financially as psychologically.

BUS DRIVER [2 47]

- Danger and obstacles are in front of you, especially because of money problems.

- Also your family life for a while will be uncertain; you may think about divorce, but most likely it will be only a thought.

BUTCHER [8 19 55]

- It is the symbol of humanity's lower instincts prevailing over reason.

- If you see him cutting meat, it means that somebody is trying to corrupt your loved one or your children if you have any.

- Only if the butcher stands outside his shop does the dream have a good meaning, and soon you may be leaving for a pleasure trip.

CARPENTER [31 50]

- It is a symbol of patience, good will, and honesty.

- To dream of a carpenter at work means a general improvement in your status.

- If you are working with a carpenter, it is a very lucky dream and you will realize that soon.

CLOWN [3 43]

- Sorrow and tears.

- Wait for a better dream if you have to start a new enterprise.

- Luck is not with you, just withdraw into yourself.

CREDITOR [13 53]

- To dream of a creditor is a bad omen.

- You are coming to a standstill, not as much financially as psychologically.

- You feel dried out and you need some kind of a shock to start your engine again.

DAUGHTER [9 41]

- To dream of your daughter signifies the end of a troublesome season. After a short period of mendingwounds, times of pleasure and harmony are beginning.

DEAD PERSON [5 47]

- Good health and long life for you, your family, and the family of the dead person.

- Monetary gains are almost sure, as is a vacation that may become longer than you thought because of a pleasing surprise.

DEVIL [22 2]

- If you dream of the devil like he is commonly represented, with horns and tail and dressed in red, your ambition is exceeding its limits. You feel almost proud of your lower instincts.

- If you dream of a normal person, knowing that in spite of the plain appearance he or she is the devil, it means that you are ashamed of the same lower instincts.

- If you fight against the devil and you win, you will overcome all obstacles and prevail over your enemies.

DOCTOR [12 38]

- Inferiority complex.

- We have been brought up very rigidly and now we are afraid of everything.

- Shyness makes it very difficult to show your feelings and too many scruples are obstacles to your activities.

DWARF [8 39]

- Good luck to you.

- Your health is very good and any physical activity required by your job is no problem at all.

- A single woman will soon meet a very interesting man.

- If you think that substance is more important than form, this is the time to get involved in a situation that soon will lead to marriage.

FARMER [12 40]

- It is symbol of loyalty, simplicity and parsimony.

- To dream of a farmer plowing a field brings good luck and prosperity, even if not real wealth.

FATHER [22 41]

- Strength and readiness to fight, but also predominance and jealousy.

- Generally the father is dreamed of much less than the mother, who means protection; but when you dream of him, it means that you did not overcome the frustration of a restrictive upbringing.

- If you dream of the father who has a loving attitude toward you, it means that you will receive good advice and should follow it. A sick father forecasts a period of unhappiness and insecurity.

FRIEND [17 19 36]

- To dream of a friend means that you talk too much.

- You should try to be more secretive: your behavior is too open and sincere, and will create only problems for you.

- We risk to endanger something important that will happen to us, like a new job or the purchase of something valuable.

GHOST [13 73 61]

- You are having problems in the family, but very soon they will vanish thanks to the intervention of true friends.

- In the specific case that you might fear losing your job, you should not worry because a better one is waiting for you.

- Same thing goes for lovers: if you should lose your partner, after a brief period of bewilderment, you will find another person more interesting than the first one.

GIANT [11 39]

- In everyday life, it is a symbol of strength and ambition, but in a dream it is a bad omen because it means that you will fail in something you were counting on very much.

- If you dream of knocking down a giant, the meaning goes back to being literal: your strength will enable you to overcome big obstacles.

GYPSY [34 43]

- There are two distinct meanings for this dream.

- If you dream of a group of gypsies, soon you will lose that rigidity of thoughts and narrow-mindedness that has characterized your life up to now, and you will become a more attractive person.

- If you dream only one gypsy, especially if he or she tries to enter in your house, you better start looking around for someone trying to deceive you.

HAIRDRESSER [6 14]

- To spend some time in a beauty parlor especially to have your hair dyed means clearly that even if you pretend to be friendly and honest with your acquaintances, you are just waiting for a good opportunity to deceive them for some personal gain.

- This is not the easiest thing to admit, but if you have the courage to be sincere with yourself, you will find that it is true.

HERMIT [11 38]

- It is a symbol of wisdom, knowledge, intuition, meditation, and truth.

- To dream of a hermit foretells a good life, with almost no strong emotions but heading toward a spiritual growth.

HORSEMAN [3 45]

- Very good dream.

- It shows strength, success, love for adventure, and generosity.

- If you are the horseman, socially you will be very successful.

- If you dream a horseman with a costume or an armor, your success will be more in the romantic field.

HUMPBACK [9 19]

- This is the time to gamble.

- If you are moderate in your betting and not too greedy, a winning is almost certain.

- Remember to stop early, though: If you insist, your luck will change.

- It is a good time also to look for a new home. You can find what you want and at an amazing price.

JUDGE [16 38]

- Because judges are thought to be honest, impartial, and stern, this dream shows all the feelings of fear and guilt of the dreamer.

- To be the judge yourself, it shows the inability to solve your own moral doubts.

KING [8 9 29]

- Honors and glory.

- Whatever is your activity—commercial, artistic or intellectual—success is guaranteed, but only if you work hard for it. In this dream there is no place for loafers.

- If you see yourself dressed as a king, it is a symbol of pride. No one can even compare to you.

- Unfortunately, soon enough you will realize that a little humility could have avoided your ostracism by the majority of your friends.

LOVER (WOMAN) [21 36]

- In a man's dream, this shows a desire to possess and exploit the opposite sex.

- Being left by a lover is a good omen. It means that the dreamer is getting rid of negative elements that were disturbing his romantic relations.

- Kissing or making love to a lover foretells the arrival of a gift or good news.

LOVER (MAN) [32 36]

- For a woman to dream of having a lover shows the wish to be protected and to find a balance in her love life.

- There is a hidden conflict between the desire to be possessed and the fear of being abandoned. It foretells a period of emotional instability.

LAWYER [26 47]

- It is the symbol of anguish, hatred, and fear of judgment, and it is a bad omen.

- There will be quarrels in the family.

- If two or more lawyers appear in the dream discussing something between them, there will be also a loss of money because of a bad investment.

MAID [2 52]

- Gossip and petty rivalry.

- Endless discussions with colleagues.

- For a while you will lose all interest in your job, at least until the situation goes back to normal.

MAIL CARRIER [22 67]

- It means confidence and responsibility.

- It foretells advancement in your career and new well-paid duties.

- If the mail person is of the opposite sex of the dreamer, his or her love life will receive a boost. A new shocking romantic encounter is near.

MOTHER [19 42 46]

- Is the symbol of affection, understanding and protection; but in a dream, represents the need of the dreamer for all three of these things.

- He or she has not yet reached the necessary maturity to face the difficulties of life.

- A mother who feeds her baby brings prosperity to the dreamer.

- And in the same way as with a father, to dream of a loving mother foretells that you will receive good advice worthy of being followed; while if you dream a sick mother, sorrow and unhappiness are ahead.

NUN [14 54]

- Humility, tolerance, order and obedience.

- For a woman, dreaming of being a nun means to be afraid of her own sexuality with consequent repression of her natural instincts.

- A nun dressed in white is a good omen and you will be successful in most of your tasks. A nun dressed in black means instead that bad luck will strike your home.

- The dream of two nuns walking together means that a lot of patience is required from you to cope with a series of small annoyances.

NURSE [27 56]

- A nurse in the house means that something will have to be healed.

- Maybe a real disease will hit you in the near future, or your feelings will be hurt.

- Seeing a nurse leave the house means good health for your family.

- For a woman to dream of being a nurse, it means that she is lacking self confidence and she needs to pretend to be something different from what she really is.

OLD MAN [8 38]

- This dream is similar to the one of the hermit.

- It shows safety, wisdom, and idealism.

- Good news will be arriving very soon; many things will be accomplished.

OLD WOMAN [9 33]

- Good health and long life.

- You cannot complain about the present. You don't regret anything belonging to the past, and you can expect a pleasant future.

- You are not really interested in wealth and you will have a comfortable life full of intimate satisfactions.

PILOT [35 51]

- It is a beautiful symbol of courage and boldness.

- The more characteristic the pilot looks— with overalls, helmet, insignia and medals—the more luck it brings.

- If on top of everything you see the pilot flying, even your most ambitious projects will succeed.

- The dream of a pilot crashing with his airplane, for obvious reasons, should be carefully avoided!

POLICEMAN [3 6 53]

- Who is the dreamer?

- For an honest person who has nothing to fear from the law, dreaming of a policeman means safety and justice, and foretells a recognition of certain virtues that will bring honors and improve the social position.

- But for somebody who has reason to feel guilty, the dream of a policeman becomes almost a nightmare and foretells a period of depression that could lead to serious financial losses.

PRIEST [3 22 69]

- People think that you really know what you are talking about.

- It does not matter if it is true or not.

- The fact is that you will be able to profit from their belief and if you play your cards right, your position on the job or in society will rise over your best expectations.

QUEEN [20 35]

- Dreaming of a queen for a man denotes his aspirations toward a fulfilling family life where his wife could successfully assume the responsibilities of the house.

- For a woman, instead there is the same danger of pride that was in the dream of the king. This pride has to be tamed if she wants respect and acceptance from her friends.

SISTER [11 32 54]

- Lucky dream for lovers.

- More for the couples that enjoy a platonic, intellectual relationship than for the ones that prefer torrid encounters.

- Engaged couples can be sure to have chosen the right mate.

- Affinity of feelings will characterize their marriage and any eventual future quarrel will not depend on lack of affection.

SOLDIER [31 45]

- It is a symbol of duty and courage but also of anger and hate.

- To dream of being a soldier is not a good dream and foretells the end of a relationship or a friendship.

- A wounded soldier means that somehow your properties will be damaged.

- The classical and ancient image of a soldier riding a horse means that your mood will change for the better and you will have good times with friends.

SON [18 31 36]

- If you dream of having a son, especially if you see him as a newborn, it means that happiness will be with you because of something new appearing in your life—a new love, a new job, or a new friend.

- Dreaming of your own son, the one you have in reality, is a bad omen and shows worries and insecurity in your romantic relationships.

TEACHER [2 39]

- Means fear and insecurity.

- You feel that your duties are too much for you.

- You do not want to face your responsibilities and your first instinct is to quit.

- To dream a music teacher with whom we are learning to play an instrument means to have the will and the patience to fight back these feelings of withdrawal.

THIEF [17 63]

- You cannot overcome your feeling of guilt.

- This puts you, in the dream and in real life, in a very uncomfortable position of inferiority.

- To be robbed by a thief means the loss of confidence in a close friend.

PLACES

Abbey
Airplane
Attic

Banquet
Bathroom
Bed
Boat
Bridge

Car
Cart
Castle
Cave
Cellar
Church
Cliff
Concert
Countryside

Desert

Elevator

Funeral

Garden

Heaven
Hell
Hospital
Hotel
House

Jail

Kitchen

Lake
Lighthouse

Market
Mill
Mountain
Movie house

Ocean

Path
Port

Restaurant
River
Ruin

Sand
School
Ship
Staircase
Store
Swamp

Theater
Throne

Well
Wood

The places where the events of the dream occur are very important.

They express the capability of the dreamer to fit comfortably in the situations of real life.

The more unknown and imaginary are the places, the more the dreamer shows the will to take shelter in a world of fantasy, refusing to accept his or her responsibilities.

Always keep in mind that the same symbol can assume a different meaning according to the way it shows itself. For example, to see a garden well kept and on a sunny day is a much better omen than to see the same garden abandoned and during a storm.

ABBEY [20 56]

- Hypocrisy and fraud.

- Someone flaunting irreproachable manners will try to cheat you.

- If you have your own business, be careful in extending credit.

- If you are elderly and not feeling well, the advice is to consult a doctor and not trust unorthodox healers.

AIRPLANE [7 36]

- It means self confidence and courage.

- If you dream of flying an airplane, you are ready to confront any danger, and since you are not afraid to take risks, you will be rewarded with a better job or position in society.

ATTIC [13 58]

- A feeling of regret and nostalgia is pervading your mood.

- You are unhappy with the way you are living your life and tend to regress to an outdated behavior that was good in the past.

- To dream about an attic foretells a loss. Somebody close to you will go far away or you will lose money in a bad investment.

BANQUET [11 44]

- You are scattering your intellectual energy in useless tasks.

- Any serious problem that should face you would find you unprepared.

- It is time to wake up to reality before it is too late.

BATHROOM [17 47]

- Repressed guilty feelings, especially in the sexual field are bothering you. Don't even try to hide them; instead do something about them.

• Basically, you are confused and lack self confidence. It will show up clearly with the opposite sex.

BED [28 49]

• No problems in the interpretation of this dream: a bed means rest and tranquillity.

• You have been working hard and now is the time to enjoy the fruits of your efforts.

• Do not be tempted to change job or residence. Stay where you are and maybe reward yourself with some deserved treat like a vacation or a gift.

BOAT [33 42]

• Unexpected visits.

• Casual meetings will become very meaningful.

• This is an important dream for those who, because of their business, meet a lot of people. It will not be difficult for you to recognize and approach somebody very important for your future.

- A half sunken boat full of water means you have to be careful of how you talk: unintentionally you may say something offensive to a new acquaintance.

BRIDGE [41 66]

- The trouble and worries that you will experience in the near future can be easily overcome; you have the ability to do so without receiving much harm.

- To cross a bridge means that these trouble and worries are gone but also that you should remember this experience to avoid something similar in the future.

CAR [27 32]

- This dream refers to the car as a status symbol.

- To drive a sports car means that you are proud and overvalue your possibilities. You risk a hard impact with reality.

- To be seated in the back of a four-door driven by a chauffeur means that you are satisfied with your achievements and don't care what other people are thinking of you.

CART [14 56]

- If this cart is pulled by oxen it has a meaning opposite to the one of the car.

- It means in fact that you are aware of what is going on around you and that you have the will and the knowledge to get to the root of a problem and solve it.

CASTLE [23 62]

- If you dream that you are living in a castle, it means that you have the tendency to withdraw from everyday life.

- Perhaps you lived some time in the past.

- The fact is that you must increase your efforts to live today without regrets. If you do, you will realize that it is not so bad after all.

CAVE [4 21 58]

- You are scared of what is going on around you and the cave is the symbol of the refuge where you would like to hide.

- Like the dream of a castle, don't let melancholic thoughts dictate your behavior. Fight back.

CELLAR [12 21 39]

- You are trying to bring to the surface feelings and thoughts you have been hiding even from yourself.

- If the cellar you are dreaming of is well lit and clean, and the stairs to get out are clearly visible, you will be successful and this will be a dream of liberation.

- If instead the cellar is dark and dirty, you will remain in a state of confusion. To get rid of these feelings and thoughts will require more pain and effort.

CHURCH [16 44]

- The meaning of this dream depends mainly on your attitude toward religious matters.

- To be in church may signify freedom from all your worries, rewards, new friendships; or could bring to the surface guilty feelings that will be an obstacle to your activities.

- In both cases, however, there is the wish of an interior search for better spiritual values.

CLIFF [22 38]

- The danger is clear.

- You are afraid to lose the place that you reached in your job or in society.

- It might be that you are aware that you got where you are not on your own merits, but from help by others.

CONCERT [3 51]

- Music has a purifying connotation.

- Seeing yourself at a concert shows your desire for harmony and order.

- Once you have brought these qualities back to your life, everything will proceed smoothly and success will be yours.

COUNTRYSIDE [14 52]

- Fertility and abundance.

- Green is the color of hope: this is a very good dream.

- Whatever you are going to start, and in particular any physical work, will be happily accomplished. You will have success, and it will bring you praise and rewards.

DESERT [7 25]

- Loneliness.

- Your love is drying up; you may lose your partner. Your bad attitude toward life will keep friends and acquaintances from you.

- You may not be strong enough to handle this situation by yourself. If this is so, don't be ashamed to look for counseling.

ELEVATOR [1 8]

- Claustrophobia: you are in a tight spot with your life.

- All your good will and efforts are not acknowledged by others.

- Make sure to dream the elevator going up: the meaning is that soon a stroke of luck will help you to get out from your struggle.

FUNERAL [8 47]

- You are tired of fighting for a modest success, and now tend toward pessimism. Do not worry, this feeling is only temporary and soon you will be confident again.

- Dreaming to be at your own funeral is a very good omen: with you will be buried all your fears and doubts. You are ready to be reborn with new courage and strength.

GARDEN [31 49]

- Relax and let the romantic side of you take over your life.

- The more flowers you see in the garden, the stronger is this need of yours to reveal certain sentimental feelings that you were almost ashamed to show.

- Let yourself go and become a better person!

HEAVEN [8 62]

- In spite of the images suggested, dreaming of heaven is not good.

- It means gossips for sure, and maybe a serious accident.

- You may lose a partner or a friendship; couples may break their engagement.

- Traveling is dangerous.

HELL [20 29]

- Your ideas are confused: you hesitate.

- When you slow your activity to try to understand what is happening around you, people think you are weak and lack even the authority to run your own family.

HOSPITAL [14 53]

- Dreaming of visiting a hospital means that you have the strength and patience to stand and react to whatever will happen to you in life.

- To dream that you are the patient in the hospital is a bad omen and indicates a sad and lonely soul.

HOTEL [23 69]

- Insecurity.

- You cannot get rid of a feeling that whatever you achieved is temporary.

- It does not matter if people have a high esteem of you and praise you for your success: until you acknowledge your own value, this feeling of dissatisfaction will not leave you.

HOUSE [13 17 43 62]

- The house is known to represent the personality of the dreamer, that is why the meaning of the dream changes according to the house that is represented.

- For example a brand new house is the symbol of a renewal in your life; a dirty and dilapidated house is a sign of unhappiness and the need to change.

JAIL [19 48]

- Dreaming of a jail means that you are putting some distance between you and others, with the result of feeling alone and isolated.

- Getting in or out of jail, therefore, shows your wish to be further or closer to the people around you.

KITCHEN [3 26 32]

- Warmth and affection.

- Your family life is fulfilling and you don't need to go out looking for something you already have in your life.

- It is a very valuable situation and a very precious feeling. Don't lose them with silly mistakes.

LAKE [18 46]

- This dream has a connotation similar to the one of the ocean, only not emphasized as much.

- To dream of a lake is a sign of interior peace and contentment.

- Fishing successfully in a lake means that good luck is coming to you in business, even more in gambling.

LIGHTHOUSE [2 20]

- It is a symbol of safety and friendship.

- Seeing the light at night is a sign of self-confidence.

- You don't refuse good advice, but you already know where you are heading and know you will be successful.

MARKET [8 21 66]

- Dreaming of a market is a very good dream for people in business: the dream is close to their real life and fits smoothly in their way of thinking.

- It foretells monetary gains.

MILL [24 43]

- The old mill on the creek is not a common sight nowadays.

- That is why seeing this mill in your dreams means that you will encounter an unusual situation at work.

- If you see the mill in function, it will be easy to face this new situation, but if you see the mill old and dilapidated, beware. The new task will require all your energy and shrewdness.

MOUNTAIN [10 50]

- If you see the mountain from a close distance, you might feel overwhelmed by the huge sight and in real life refuse to accept an offer that you think is beyond your possibilities.

- If you are climbing the mountain or are already on top, nothing could stop you in your progress.

- Artists will ignore nasty judgments made by self-appointed critics.

MOVIE HOUSE [12 23 52]

- When you watch a movie in your waking state, you forget what is going on outside, and this is also the meaning of the dream.

- You are in a period of stagnation and you would rather lose yourself in daydreaming than face the daily routine.

- If you have the time and money, you should go away soon for a trip or a cruise, but maybe you can compromise. What about a weekend far enough away from your boring surroundings?

OCEAN [16 28 63]

- It means rest and peace.

- Most of your wishes will have a positive answer.

- If the ocean is agitated but the sky is clear, you are going to meet new friends, maybe a new love.

- If the weather is stormy, with big waves and a dark sky, the dream foretells some accident that will hit you or someone very close to you.

PATH [4 43]

- By the way this path looks, you will be able to tell how your life will unfold in the immediate future for a short period of time.

- Walking on a narrow and muddy path means that some annoying trouble will slow your progress; a large and comfortable path instead is the sign that everything will go smoothly for you.

PORT [30 56]

- The meaning of this dream varies depending on if you are entering the port, or if you are sailing out from it.

- In the first case you have no doubts about whatever you are doing and you have plenty of self-confidence.

- The opposite happens in the second case. You have serious decisions to make, and may not have enough information about the matter. The risk involved makes you uncomfortable.

RESTAURANT [11 55]

- You are not familiar with the food you are eating.

- A period of anxiety is ahead of you.

- This is not necessarily a bad dream: it warns you to be careful about a situation that will require all your attention.

RIVER [3 18 48]

- Somehow the river is the mirror of your life.

- A peaceful river with clear water means that your life will be calm and successful.

- A running river with murky water foretells danger, especially in business.

- A river interrupted by a waterfall announces that something unexpected but pleasurable will happen to you.

RUINS [7 59]

- They announce the end of an old way of thinking and the beginning of a new.

- The transition will happen smoothly but will require a considerable amount of time.

- The result nevertheless will be one hundred percent positive.

SAND [2 16 50]

- This is not the time for starting anything new.

- Life is dragging. Keep yourself strictly to routine.

- You are lucky if you are able to carry on in a decent way whatever you have already started.

SCHOOL [28 29]

- Be ready for disturbing events.

- Lack of information will cause you to make serious mistakes.

- Don't trust your judgment. Look for professional help: it may be that it's your only way out.

SHIP [5 31]

- To dream of a cargo ship means that you are feeling the weight of your responsibilities. You will come out from a bad situation, but it will cost you much aggravation.

- If you dream instead of taking a cruise on a ship full of happy people, it means that you are prepared for your trip through life and will sail smoothly with the blessings of your family and friends.

STAIRCASE [23 36]

- As you can imagine, the key of this dream is if you are going up or down the stairs.

- You gain if you go up; you lose if you go down. Hold onto the rail, because if you dream you are falling down the stairs, you will meet serious financial losses.

STORE [13 52]

- A store full of goods means prosperity for the dreamer, and the opposite if the store is empty.

- To sell merchandise in a store means that your efforts will be rewarded.

- To buy goods means you know you are lacking qualities necessary to succeed.

- Another meaning of the dream is linked to the kind of merchandise sold or bought in the store.

SWAMP [4 12]

- Obstacles.

- It is up to you to go ahead with a project; the probability of success is 50/50.

- Maybe some other element in the dream could help you in your decision.

THEATER [16 22 49]

- If you dream of being the spectator, it could mean deception. Don't trust the loyalty of a person of the opposite sex.

- Avoid getting involved.

- If you dream of being the actor, it means that something you will do in the near future will bring you honor and rewards.

THRONE [8 23]

- It shows a secret need you have to over-shadow others.

- This feeling might help you in some big achievement, but could also show a proud side of your nature that does not make you very popular.

WELL [17 35 62]

- It symbolizes the front you put out to cover feelings you are not very proud of and that you would rather keep hidden.

- Pulling water from a well means that you are making an effort to get rid of these shameful feelings.

- Falling in the well means that you give in to these feelings and show an ugly side of your nature. You will lose dear friends.

WOOD [9 41]

- The key of this dream is not to get lost in the woods.

- If you walk among the trees following a path in daytime, it means that you know what is good for you and sooner or later you will get it.

- Walking in the woods at night is a bad omen. You may easily become scared and what looked so close before, now is almost impossible to reach.

PLANTS, FLOWERS, AND FRUITS

Apple
Apricot
Artichoke
Azalea

Basil
Bean
Blackberry

Camellia
Cherry
Chestnut
Clover

Eucalyptus

Fig
Fir
Four-leaf
  clover

Gardenia
Geranium
Garlic
Grape

Jasmine

Laurel
Lemon
Lily

Mint
Melon

Oak
Olive
Orange

Palm
Peach

Pear
Pine
Pineapple
Plum
Poppy
Potato

Rose
Rosemary

Sage
Strawberry

Tree
Tulip

Vineyard
Violet

Walnut

Whatever belongs to the vegetable world, especially flowers, indicates a calm and peaceful soul, almost perfectly at ease in the environment.

Taken one by one, though, each plant, fruit, and flower can take different meanings.

APPLE [9 23]

- In your dream, this fruit is the symbol of family unity.

- Togetherness is the password.

- If you pick it from the tree still unripe, little quarrels will disturb your peace, but when you see it ripe and red, everything is happening for the best.

APRICOT [27 37 4]

- Dreaming of apricots makes you aware of a great passion burning inside you; but it is so difficult for you to manifest your feelings that this passion will be more of a pain than a joy.

ARTICHOKE [42 45 12]

- In the end, you will succeed in whatever you undertake, but be ready to overcome many obstacles that will put your patience to a test.

AZALEA [12 19]

- Bad dream for lovers.

- Your needs and your desires for physical love are going to be frustrating.

- Look for a new relationship as soon as possible.

BASIL [37 16]

- Dreaming of basil, especially if you can smell it, is a bad omen for your mental health.

- You may go through a long period of depression that will change your whole personality.

BEANS [36 14]

- In the past, beans were believed to protect people from ghosts and evil spirits.

- If you dream about them you can be sure someone is gossiping about you.

- Don't try to correct this situation, you may make things worst.

- Whoever knows you will not believe these lies anyway.

BLACKBERRY [42 11 32]

- Don't trust the person you love.

- You have been told a bunch of lies and you believed everything.

- This naiveté will cause you a lot of pain.

CAMELLIA [30 22]

- Just the opposite of blackberries.

- These flowers are the symbol of a great love and much happiness.

- If in the dream your lover gives you one, his or her love is strong, passionate, and will last forever.

CHERRIES [48 2 49 3]

- If you dream of picking them from the tree, you will have a fight with one of your closest friends.

- But if you dream of eating them, you can expect good news and joy.

CHESTNUT [36 25]

- Everything is going smoothly for you.

- All your wishes will be satisfied, including one that you don't dare tell anyone.

- Try to carry a chestnut in your right pocket and see how luck will follow you wherever you go.

CLOVER [33 16 3]

- You will fall in love very soon, but this time the feeling will be more tender and sentimental than hot and passionate.

EUCALYPTUS [38 30]

- Has been used in the past to fight the evil eye.

- It is a symbol of sincere feelings and honesty.

- Will bring good luck in your business enterprises.

FIG [4 22]

- Sadness and unhappiness.
- If you dream of figs, you will wake up with a sense of doom that will be with you at least for a week.

FIR [24 15 5]

- If you dream of only one tree, you tap the melancholic joy of Christmas.
- A whole forest fills your heart with sadness, and the darker the forest, the sadder your thoughts will be in the morning.

FOUR LEAF CLOVER [5 8]

- Wrong guess!
- Dreaming a four-leaf clover does not bring luck like finding one.
- It increases your capability of enjoying

the company of different people. Your social life will expand toward new areas that you thought were out of your reach.

GARDENIA [37 23]

- Hot passion is ahead.

- Get ready to be involved in a short but intense romantic relationship.

- Something that you did not expect will happen and that will leave you breathless.

GERANIUM [36 9 1]

- Beware!

- Smart and dishonest people will try to cheat you and, unfortunately, they will have good chances of succeeding.

GARLIC [24 31]

- No matter the effort you put in your work, certain unpleasant situations, especially in business, will remain static.

- Be ready for anxiety.

GRAPE [4 8 29]

- If you see it still hanging in the vineyard, don't expect any important change in your life.

- If you eat it, every mouthful will bring new goodies for you—new friendships, new money, and new love.

JASMINE [35 22 6]

- Somebody is secretly in love with you but does not have the courage to tell you.

- It is up to you to find out, and if you are interested, give him or her a little help.

LAUREL [28 9 10]

- For laurel, you can refer to what was said previously about geranium.

- But this time you will be able to get your revenge.

LEMON [22 1 16]

- You will be caught by surprise with bad news.

- Unfortunately, you will not be able to react immediately in the right way, and serious damage will follow.

LILY [10 4]

- This flower is a symbol of purity.

- It was said that it could keep bad forces away from people.

- When you dream about lilies, it means that you are aware of a hidden dark side of your personality but you know how to fight back and keep this side of yours under control.

MINT [20 2]

- Don't trust anyone.

- A person close to you will try to take advantage of your lack of experience in financial matters, and great damage could follow.

MELON [2 30 31]

- Success.

- You will succeed in everything you want to do, and more so if you invented something useful.

- Don't waste any time in having it patented, and look for someone who will help you in merchandising your gadget.

OAK [32 6 41]

- Luck follows you everywhere.

- It will not take you long to realize that everything is unfolding very easily in your life, and you will be the first one to be surprised.

- Relax and enjoy.

OLIVE [14 16 9]

- This is the time to gamble.

- Go to Las Vegas if you can, otherwise go to the Monday night bingo of your church, but don't miss this occasion.

Bring a big bag with you!

ORANGE [10 32 6]

- Certain people believe that the flower of the orange tree means purity, and that is why they use it to make the bouquet for the new bride.

- Whatever you dream of the flower or the fruit, you can expect a beautiful gift.

PALM [1 34 9]

- You can refer to what has been written for the oak.

- On top of that, you will be sheltered against any form of gossip.

PEACH [22 24]

- Any time you dream of this fruit, something bad will happen.

- It depends on who you are or what you are doing, but you may have big losses in business, get seriously ill, or see the end of a sentimental relationship.

PEAR [9 38 7]

- Very similar to the peach, but with this fruit, the accent is definitely on money.

- The losses may be so big that you are risking real poverty.

PINE [31 8]

- Your household and family environment is deteriorating very quickly.

- You will be concerned with the behavior of your wife or your children.

- It is time to make serious decisions.

PINEAPPLE [17 33 14]

- Good dream.

- You can count on the best results for anything you will be willing to start.

- This will be particularly true for intellectual matters.

PLUM [3 17 37]

- If you dream of this fruit, your love life is literally going to pieces.

- You realize how difficult it is for you to keep alive a romantic relationship.

- Maybe is time to change partners.

POPPY [30 7]

- You are too naive.

- You have been trusting a person who in a short time will prove to be anything but a real friend.

- Unfortunately, by that time it will be too late for you to avoid the damage.

POTATO [4 8 14]

- This dream foretells many problems on the job.

- Nothing really serious or that you cannot solve, but something that will take a lot of time from things that are more important.

ROSE [13 18 24]

- Very good dream for engaged couples.

- A problem that could have delayed the marriage, maybe finding a house or a job, gets happily solved with the intervention of a family member.

ROSEMARY [9 19]

- People around the Mediterranean Sea in the ancient times used to give this plant to newlyweds to be remembered through the years.

- In a dream it has a strong positive meaning still in the sphere of love; in fact it stands for the confidence and love that your partner has for you.

SAGE [4 22]

- It's a great dream, especially in the field of health.

- It foretells a period free from any disease.

- Even that little pain you experienced lately will soon disappear.

STRAWBERRY [31 14]

- This dream shows your good heart and wisdom.

- You can expect help from a person who recognizes your values and appreciates them.

TREE [20 14 15 13]

- When you dream about a generalized tree, it means you don't have enough confidence in yourself.

- The trees give fruits (nutrition) and wood (heat). These are symbols of the understanding you want from the people around you.

TULIP [33 5]

- Dreaming of a tulip, for both men and women, means they are aware of their ability to attract and seduce members of the opposite sex.

- This activity can give them satisfaction, but also a lot of trouble.

VINEYARD [25 8]

- Like the sage, this is a symbol of good health.

- All your ailments will disappear and you will feel as strong and energetic as if you were ten years younger.

VIOLET [3 29]

- Dream of this flower if you are an artist.

- Painters, sculptors, and whoever expresses his or her artistic temperament by drawing, will be acknowledged.

- Financial recognition will also follow.

WALNUT [12 36]

- The meaning of this dream is surprise.

- Something that you did not expect will happen.

- There is no need to worry because it will be a nice surprise, most likely concerning money.

PRECIOUS STONES AND JEWELS

Amber
Amethyst

Bracelet

Coral

Diamond

Emerald

Gold

Necklace

Onyx
Pearl

Ring
Ruby

Sapphire
Silver

Topaz
Turquoise

Man has always been charmed by precious stones.

Because of the difficulty of finding them and transforming them into jewels, they have been considered a symbol of wealth and power.

It has been said that they offer healing and magic virtues to whomever owns them.

AMBER [16 41]

- Dreaming amber is a good omen for health.

- For a long time you will not be sick.

- It could mean also that you will receive favors from unselfish friends and your income will grow.

AMETHYST [19 32]

- It is a potent talisman for love matters.

- If you dream it, even your most daring wish could come true.

- Generally speaking, it foretells success in all fields of life.

BRACELET [20 50]

- Your hands are tied.

- Many obstacles are in the way of your actions.

- Stick to the usual routine.

- Don't try to help your friends; any help will make them resentful.

CORAL [3 32 51]

- It is a bad omen stone.

- Foretells danger for whomever dreams it or for loved ones.

- Some people, nevertheless, use it as an amulet to protect themselves from danger related to the ocean.

DIAMOND [26 61]

- This stone gives good health and encourages people to get married.

- If you dream of it, your love will be reciprocated and business matters will be smooth and successful.

EMERALD [4 19]

- Is considered the best talisman by the sailors and the high sea fishermen.

- To give it to a lover is a symbol of faithfulness.

- To dream of this stone means that you are trusted in business and in love.

GOLD [5 49]

- Is the greatest dream for a single woman: very soon she will meet her soul mate.

- If you see yourself wearing a lot of gold, you want to satisfy all your desires, no matter what they cost.

- In general, after you dream of gold, your wealth is going to increase.

NECKLACE [34 44]

- By itself, it is a symbol of greed and stinginess.

- But with something hanging from it, like a cross, stone, or medallion, it signifies faith and confidence.

- Be careful to put your trust in something worthwhile and not in a fad.

ONYX [31 39]

- Humility is the symbol of this stone. Your spirituality is increasing, and you are less attached to worldly matters.

- A subtle change is happening to you, but it is still at the early stage and is difficult to perceive.

PEARL [7 48]

- Pearls represent tears.
- Your luck is vanishing.
- Don't do anything important for a while.
- Some people believe that pearls should be given only to single women.
- Married women would get only bad luck from them.

RING [22 52]

- You are tied up.
- Something is controlling your love life or maybe you don't feel free to act the way you want in business.

- You need help to get out of this situation. You will get it, but it will cost you dearly.

RUBY [4 26 48]

- Wear it in a dangerous situation.

- It will protect you from the snares of envious people.

- Watch it carefully; it is said to change color when something bad is approaching.

- If you dream of it, it foretells hot passion with a very uncertain end.

SAPPHIRE [12 36]

- If you dream of it, people around you will acknowledge all your good qualities, especially spirituality.

- In fact, this stone is a symbol of purifying thoughts.

SILVER [13 63]

- Nothing is enough for you.

- You keep looking for something new, but whatever you find is unsatisfactory.

- You are too attached to material pleasures, and only when you realize where the real values are will you find peace.

TOPAZ [16 47]

- This is the stone to wear if you are afraid of the evil eye.

- Nothing is stronger for protection.

- If you dream of it, you will overcome hateful and envious people around you.

TURQUOISE [13 25]

- Your friends can trust you; you are loyal and faithful to them.

- You are shrewd in business and economics.

- It can also protect you from evil spirits.

SKY AND ELEMENTS

Cloud

Day or night

Earth
Earthquake
Eclipse

Fire
Fog

Hail

Lightning

Moon

Planet

Rainbow

Snow
Star
Storm
Sun

Thunder

Water
Wind

Both the sky and the elements are very important reference points in the history of humanity.

From the beginning, in fact, man has based his farming and his ability to sail on the knowledge of the skies.

The four basic elements of air, water, fire and earth—besides being thought by some ancient philosopher to be at the base of the structure of the universe—are the only sure things that have allowed the survival of the human race.

CLOUD [20]

- If they are white, there will be all kinds of happiness for you.

- But from pale grey to black, things are going from bad to worse.

- It will be very difficult for your plans to succeed or maybe they won't succeed at all.

- You may be cheated in buying some product for the house.

DAY OR NIGHT [12 31 1 10]

- Whatever you dream can happen in daylight or at night (it doesn't matter if you dream it at night or during an afternoon nap).

- If it happens in daylight, it has more probability to come true, and more so if the sun is shining.

- There are two special numbers to take into consideration: 1 for the day, and 10 for the night.

EARTH OR SKY [13 43]

- The fact is that whatever you dream can happen while you have your two feet on the ground or while you are floating in the air.

- There are two special numbers for this situation, too: 13 for the earth and 43 for the sky.

EARTHQUAKE [44 43 4]

- Two kinds of people are in danger if they dream of an earthquake: those who own businesses must be very careful not to lose their credit; and pregnant women should avoid any physical stress so that they don't lose their babies.

ECLIPSE [7 13 30]

- Treachery and infidelity, in business and in love.

- If you are in business, your partner or close assistant is ready to deceive you. Try to unmask him before it is too late.

- If you travel a lot or you often leave your partner alone, be aware that someone is ready to take her or him away from you, and with good probabilities of success.

FIRE [29 2 14]

- Dreaming of fire has at least three different meanings: erotic passion, knowledge, and mirth.

- Sometimes can be contradictory—you have to decide which is the right meaning according to the circumstances of the dream.

- Just keep in mind that lighting a fire means a wish to change; putting it out is self-wounding; getting burned means risk and danger.

FOG [19 6]

- Dissatisfaction and sadness.

- It is time to understand that you cannot have everything in life. Be happy with what you have.

- To get lost in the fog means some small financial loss or foretells some minor disease.

- But seeing the fog fading away confirms that any major decision you made was the right one.

HAIL [21 3]

- Bad news.

- Something painful will happen in the near future.

- Your romantic life is threatened.

- Most likely someone close to you will take away your loved one.

- There is also the risk that you will have to give up something that took a lot of effort for you to build.

LIGHTNING [10 21]

- If you see lightning strike, it means fear of something negative. It will most likely happen on the job.

- If you or your house are struck by the lightning, that is really good luck for you, maybe in business, definitely in gambling.

MOON [3 19]

- The Lady of the Night is the symbol of femininity, with all the qualities and the faults that folk wisdom ascribes to women.

- If a woman dreams of the moon, it means that she is trying to compensate for her alleged lack of femininity.

- But if a man has this dream, it means that he is psychologically well balanced.

- If you dream a hazy moon, you may get sick in the near future, but if the moon is clear and sparkling, a new baby will join your family soon.

- Finally, if the moon is full, a new love will be born very soon.

RAINBOW [37 8 9]

- Gains and wealth.

- You may win at gambling, receive an inheritance, or get any kind of lucky strike.

- It is a very good time for traveling.

- The relationship with your children is going to improve.

SNOW [17 8 37]

- Chastity and purity.

- But also plentifulness.

- Beautiful dream for farmers. The crop for the next two years will be above average.

- To dream a huge snowfall means you will be making lots of money.

- To dream that you play in the snow means you will overcome any attempt of being hurt by envious people.

STAR [5 26]

- Spirituality, peace of mind, and hope.

- You may feel the wish to look into religious matters that you have neglected up to now. Someone will make fun of you because of this feeling, but the majority will praise you.

- If you dream of falling stars and you are engaged, you will get married within the year.

STORM [22 4 34]

- Success after a struggle.

- To be in the storm implies going through difficulties, but without fail, after the storm, the sun comes back out to shine.

- And the storm may be scary but never lasts too long.

SUN [8 17 22]

- Dreaming of the sunrise means that you will reach prosperity even if you will have to work hard for it.

- The sunset is a symbol of satisfaction of the position you reached. You will not be able to go much further.

- To see the sun shining high or to see it coming in from a window means your income is going to rise consistently.

THUNDER [30 8]

- It is an auditory dream, different from the majority of dreams that usually are associated with something visual.

- This dream is an invitation to young couples to conceive a child. Further delay will deprive them of joys that will lose intensity with the passing of time.

WATER [4 11 41]

- If it is clear like in a spring, the middle of the ocean, or a mountain lake, it is a symbol of good family relationships, plentifulness, and wealth.

- If murky and muddy, there is the possibility of a member of the family getting sick.

- If it flows with violence like in a flood, it means uncontrollable power. Your own excessive pride will end up ruining you.

WIND [3 23 45]

- Fear, doubt, and repentance.

- You may pay dearly for an injustice you made in the past.

- If you are about to buy something important, like a house, a car or a jewel, don't rush into it.

- You might have to change your mind when it is too late.

- If you dream of a light breeze, something new will happen in your love life.

- If the wind is strong, what you thought was a good friendship will collapse with a big fight.

About the Author

Raoul Maltagliati was born some time ago in Florence, Italy. His education at school was mainly humanistic (Italian, Latin, ancient Greek, philosophy, history). This prepared him for the studies in psychology, cultural anthropology, parapsychology, and Eastern philosophies and religions which he has pursued throughout his life.

His previous writing consists of essays for an Italian specialized magazine. One was about the faith healers and psychic surgeons of the Philippines where he went to study their activities in their own environment, along with a team of Italian scientists. Another dealt with a case of demonic possession and related exorcism of a woman in a small town in central Italy.

In his first full-length book, Maltagliati has written in an easy and amusing style, being aware that its implications are more serious than they appear to be.

To Write to the Author

If you wish to contact the author or would like more information about this book, please write to the author in care of Llewellyn Worldwide and we will forward your request. Both the author and publisher appreciate hearing from you and learning of your enjoyment of this book and how it has helped you. Llewellyn Worldwide cannot guarantee that every letter written to the author can be answered, but all will be forwarded. Please write to:

Raoul Maltagliati
c/o Llewellyn Worldwide
P.O. Box 64383-483, St. Paul, MN 55164-0383,
U.S.A.

Please enclose a self-addressed, stamped envelope for reply, or $1 to cover costs. If outside U.S.A., enclose international postal reply coupon.